FROM T[HIS]
TO COLOR

TRACING AND COLORING BOOK

Flowers

Enigma Color

super EASY

Dear Reader,

We want to extend our heartfelt gratitude for choosing our coloring book. Knowing that you've chosen to immerse yourself in our creative pages brings us immense joy.

Your support means the world to us, and we would love to hear your thoughts about your experience with the book. If you could take a moment to share your feedback on Amazon, it would be an incredibly appreciated gesture. Your words can guide other art and color enthusiasts in their book selection.

To leave a review, simply visit the book's page on Amazon and look for the review section. Your feedback is vital to our growth and ongoing improvement.

Thank you again for being a part of our creative community and for allowing us to be a part of your artistic journey.

With gratitude,
Enigma Color

Remember, authenticity and genuine gratitude are essential in your message.

Here are recommendations for painting a Tracing and coloring book:

- **Create a Relaxing Environment: Set aside a tranquil and comfortable space for coloring. Ensure it's well-lit and free from distractions.**

- **Disconnect from the Digital World: To fully immerse yourself in the coloring experience, disconnect from electronic devices.**

- **Tracing Materials: Use pencils, black ink pens, or fine markers to trace the design lines. These materials will provide precise strokes.**

- **Concentration and Relaxation: Focus on the design you're tracing and let the activity be relaxing. Don't rush; take your time for accurate tracing.**

- **Follow the Lines: Trace the lines carefully, following the design's cues. Don't worry if you make mistakes; creativity is unique!**

- **Blank Spaces: In addition to tracing lines, you'll find blank spaces for coloring. Use your favorite colors and add your personal touch.**

Keep in mind that the primary objective is to relax and relish the creative process. Don't fret too much about the final outcome. Have fun and let your creativity flow freely

"Consistency is the compass of success"

"Never stop, always move forward"

"Small victories lead to great achievements"

"Determination is the key to progress"

"Every effort brings you closer to your goals"

"Resilience is the bridge to your dreams "

"Patience opens all
doors"

"Success is the reward of the persistent"

"Keep your eyes on the prize and keep going"

"Difficulties are opportunities in disguise"

"The hardest road often leads to the greatest triumphs"

"Persistence is the secret of personal growth"

"Bold goals require bold determination"

"Obstacles are just steps on the path"

"The thousand-mile journey begins with a single step"

"Don't give up; the miracle may be just around the corner"

"Perseverance turns dreams into reality"

"Unwavering
will is a superpower"

"Every setback brings you one step closer to success"

"Resilience is the force behind accomplishments"

"Adversities forge character"

"Perseverance is the key to unlock all doors"

"Never let anything
hold you back"

"Determination is the torch that lights the way"

"Success only waits
for those who keep
"
going

"Challenges are lessons in disguise"

"Resilience is the heart of perseverance"

"Every setback is a growth opportunity"

"Inner strength never gives up"

"Bold goals require bold commitment"

"Perseverance is the key to all achievements"

"Time and perseverance conquer all things"

" Struggles make you
stronger "

"Perseverance turns dreams into plans"

"Every effort counts"

"The path to success is paved with obstacles"

"The courage to keep moving forward is the engine of success"

"Setbacks are just stops on the journey"

"Persistence is the journey to success"

"Perseverance is the
light in the darkness"

Made in the USA
Las Vegas, NV
26 December 2024

15402742R00048